SAM HOUSTON
AMERICAN HERO

SAM HOUSTON

AMERICAN HERO

by Ann Fears Crawford

Illustrated by Betsy Warren

EAKIN PRESS

FIRST EDITION

Published in the United States of America
By Eakin Press, P.O. Box 23069, Austin, Texas 78735

ISBN 0-89015-644-1

Library of Congress Cataloging-in-Publication Data

Crawford, Ann Fears.
    Sam Houston: American Hero / by Ann Fears Crawford: Illustrated by
Betsy Warren.
        p.   cm.
    Bibliography: p.
    Summary: A biography of Sam Houston, first president of the Texas Re-
public, later its senator and governor, and always its hero.
    ISBN 0-89015-644-1 : $10.95
    1. Houston, Sam, 1793–1863 — Juvenile literature. 2. Texas — Gover-
nors — Biography — Juvenile literature. 3. Legislators — United States —
Biography — Juvenile literature. 4. United States. Congress. Senate — Biog-
raphy — Juvenile literature. [1. Houston, Sam, 1793–1863. 2. Statesmen.]
I. Warren, Betsy, Ill.   II. Title.
F390.H84C73 1988
976.4'04'0924 — dc19
[B]   88-3565
                              CIP
                                                                  AC

2

for

Darby and Emily Taylor
and
Timothy Houston and John Price Daniel
young Houstons and proud Texans

DREAMS OF ADVENTURE

Young Sam Houston stood on the top of a high hill. He shaded his eyes. As far as he could see, the land stretched westward.

Young Sam dreamed of the West. He loved his mother, his brothers, and his little sisters.

But he hated school. He hated helping his brothers in the store. Sam Houston yearned for adventure.

Young Sam missed his father. When the family lived in Virginia, Major Houston was often away. He found adventure with the militia.

Now Major Houston was dead. But young Sam longed to follow in his footsteps.

His mother had moved the family to Tennessee. She wanted Sam to go to school.

Still the fire of adventure burned in young Sam. He loved to read books about heroes.

Who wanted to add up sums when you could read about adventures? Who wanted to sit in school when you could run through the woods?

Sam's brothers put him to work in their store. Sam waited on customers. Flour, potatoes, and cornmeal were just as boring as school. Who wanted to be a storekeeper?

WITH THE INDIANS

One day Sam was sweeping the floor. Round and round he went with the broom. Dust flew. Cobwebs fell.

Suddenly, Sam Houston threw down the broom. He had to get away. He ran from the store and headed for the woods.

Freedom was what he wanted. Freedom to breathe the air. Freedom to read his adventure stories. Freedom to live.

Sam headed for an island in the Tennessee River. The Cherokee Indians lived there.

The chief of the Cherokees was John Jolly. He greeted Sam with kind words. He treated Sam like a son. He called him by an Indian name. Sam Houston's new name was "The Raven."

Sam found adventure with the Cherokees. He dressed in Indian clothes. He let his hair grow long.

He fished and hunted. He played stick and ball games with the Indian braves.

Nights were times for dreams. He sat around the Indian campfire. He listened to Indian tales. He dreamed dreams.

Sam even had his own "medicine animal" — the eagle. Where the eagle flew, Sam Houston followed.

After three years with the Indians, Sam had to go home. He owed people money there.

He had to make money. Sam decided to teach school.

People laughed. Imagine Sam Houston teaching school!

But the people came. They filled his split-log benches. Soon Sam's debts were paid.

War!

Then one day a man on horseback rode by the schoolhouse. "War! War!" he shouted.

Once again Sam Houston heard the call of adventure.

The army came to Tennessee. They wanted young men to join. They marched through the town. Flags flew! Drums rolled!

Sam Houston picked up a silver dollar from the drum. That meant he would join.

Now he was a member of the United States Army. He was off to fight the Creek Indians with General Andy Jackson.

Sam's mother was sorry to see him go. But she gave Sam his father's musket.

Then she slipped a ring from her finger. Inside was one word — "Honor."

She gave the ring to Sam. "Make me proud of you," she told him.

General Jackson's army moved out. The Creeks must be beaten.

Ensign Sam Houston led his men into battle. Muskets fired! Arrows flew! Over the ramparts went Jackson's men.

Suddenly, Sam felt pain in his leg. An Indian arrow had hit him.

"Pull it out!" he shouted.

One of the soldiers pulled the arrow. Sam groaned. The soldier pulled again.

Out came the arrow! But it left a bloody wound. Army doctors bandaged Sam's leg.

Then General Jackson rode up. He ordered Sam to stay in the camp. No more battles for Sam Houston.

But the Creeks refused to give up. They fought on and on.
Then General Jackson rode to the front of his army.

"Charge!" he shouted.

Suddenly, Sam Houston rose to his feet.

"Charge!" he echoed. His men followed.

Sam aimed his musket. The Indians fired back. Sam was hit
again. His arm felt like fire. His shoulder ached.

Sam dropped his musket. His men ran for cover.

General Jackson shouted an order. His men set fire to arrows. Soon flaming arrows flew into the enemy camp.

The Creeks knew they were beaten. Jackson's army had won the Battle of Horseshoe Bend.

But Sam Houston lay dying.

Jackson's army was on the move. Sam Houston was near death. They had to leave him behind.

Then soldiers from Tennessee made a bed for him. They carried Sam home.

Sam's mother took care of him. Soon he was well. Now, at last, he had time to read his books.

Then General Jackson called him back to action.

A HARD TASK

This time the job was not a battle. But it was a hard task for Sam.

General Jackson gave the orders. Sam had to persuade the Indians to move westward. The white men wanted their lands.

Houston dressed in buckskins. He threw his Indian blanket over his shoulders.

"The Raven" went back to his tribe.

Sam told Chief Jolly the Indians had to move. The Indians were sad. But they began the journey. They moved across the Mississippi River.

Then Sam went to Washington. He went to plead for the Cherokees. The government promised them money. But none came.

Sam took the Indians to see the secretary of war. The Indians left with only corn to plant and more promises.

The secretary turned on Sam. He raged at him.

"Never enter my office again. You look like a savage!" he told him.

Sam stormed out. He slammed the door. Then he quit the army. Sam Houston went back to Tennessee.

CONGRESS

Sam had to find work. Once again he owed money.

Sam decided to be a lawyer. He studied hard. He worked long hours. In six months he was a Tennessee lawyer.

Then he began to give speeches. He made many friends. They wanted him to run for public office.

Sam Houston knew his destiny. And he had a strong friend. Andrew Jackson wanted to be president of the United States.

Sam visited Jackson's home. It was called the Hermitage. The two men talked about Sam's future.

They talked about the West. Did Sam's destiny lay there? Many people were moving west. Maybe Sam's destiny lay in a new land called Texas!

First, Jackson wanted Sam to run for public office. He helped Sam become a member of the United States Congress.

Sam went to Congress from Tennessee. There he could help Jackson become president.

TENNESSEE'S GOVERNOR

Then Sam made a mistake. He fought a duel. He wounded a man.

But people in Tennessee took Sam's side. They thought he was a hero. They wanted him to be their governor. Sam went out to get votes.

People were talking about Sam Houston. They liked his speeches. And they liked his clothes. He wore ruffled shirts and a tall, beaver hat. He wore fancy breeches and leather boots.

In 1828 two Tennessee heroes were in office. Andrew Jackson was president of the United States. And Sam Houston was governor of Tennessee.

Then Sam fell in love. He thought Eliza Allen loved him too. Soon they were married.

But Eliza was very young. She was unhappy with Sam. She went back to live with her family.

Sam tried to see Eliza. But she would not see him.

Sam was very sad. He knew he could no longer be governor of Tennessee. Sam went back to live with the Indians.

BACK TO THE INDIANS

Once again Sam Houston was "The Raven." He wore Indian clothes. He wore beads on his shirt and feathers on his head.

Sam smoked the peace pipe with his Indian brothers. Then he married Tiana Rogers. She was a proud Indian woman. And she was Chief Jolly's niece.

Sam wrote to Andrew Jackson. He told him about the Indians. He told him about Texas.

Texas was a new land in the West. Now it belonged to Mexico. But some Texans wanted it to be part of the United States.

Sam Houston decided to go to Texas. He dreamed of his destiny in Texas.

Tiana had to make a choice. She wanted to stay with her people.

Sam was sad to leave the Indians. He was very sad to leave Tiana. But he gave her their house and land.

Sam Houston was off to Texas!

ROAD TO WAR

Sam Houston came to Texas at an exciting time.

In 1832 Texas belonged to Mexico. But Texans wanted to be free. They wanted to make their own laws. Some Texans wanted war.

Sam Houston was a lawyer. But soon he went to meetings with other Texans.

"War! War!" one group shouted.

"Keep the peace!" others warned.

Many Texans were mad at Santa Anna. He was the ruler of Mexico. He wanted Texas for Mexico. But Texans wanted to be free.

Santa Anna would not let Texans govern themselves. He would not let Texans make their own laws.

More and more people wanted land in Texas. "No!" said Santa Anna.

Soon the Texans declared war. "Down with Santa Anna!" they shouted. "Texas for Texans!"

THE ALAMO

The Texans chose Sam Houston to lead their army. But what an army it was!

Sam drilled his men. He wanted to wait. His army had no guns. They needed supplies.

But one group of Texans wouldn't wait. They wanted the Mexicans out of San Antonio.

The Texans fought hard. The Mexicans would not give up.

The Texans charged again and again. They won the battle.

The Mexicans were beaten this time. But Santa Anna's army was marching to Texas.

Texans thought they had won a great battle. "The war is over!" they shouted. "We won! We won!"

"Not so!" said Sam Houston. He knew he had to beat Santa Anna. Then Texas would be free.

Sam Houston sent orders to his men.

"Be quick!" he told James Fannin. "The Mexicans are coming. Leave Goliad."

"Leave San Antonio," he told Jim Bowie. "Blow up the forts. Head for open country."

But Sam Houston's plans did not work. Jim Bowie did not blow up the forts.

He and Buck Travis hurried to an old church. People in San Antonio called it the Alamo.

Other Texans joined them. Then Travis wrote a letter. He asked the people for help. He called for men to fight for Texas.

Newspapers printed the letter. Many people read about Texas and the Texans. Some wanted to join the fight.

Into the Alamo marched Davy Crockett in his coonskin cap. He brought men from Tennessee.

Other men came. They came for adventure. They came for glory. They dreamed of land for themselves. And they dreamed of freedom for Texas.

"We will never retreat!" said Buck Travis.

"We will never give up!" echoed Bowie.

"We will win!" shouted Davy Crockett.

"We will fight to the death!" said Santa Anna. "And take no prisoners."

The Mexican soldiers cut off escape from the Alamo. Then they attacked.

The Texans fought and fought. They fought bravely for thirteen days.

Then the Mexicans broke through. They raised ladders. Over the walls they went!

The Texans fought harder. Muskets fired! Knives slashed!

One Mexican soldier killed Jim Bowie. Then Davy Crockett fell.

Soon all the brave Texans lay dead. Santa Anna won the battle! The Alamo was his!

THE ROAD TO SAN JACINTO

Many Texas settlers were afraid. They heard about the fall of the Alamo. Texas was lost!

Some packed up. They began to leave Texas. Over the Sabine River lay safety.

Sam Houston heard the news. The Alamo had fallen!

A rider brought more news. The Mexicans had attacked Goliad. Fannin and his men lay dead.

"Remember the Alamo!" soldiers shouted.

"Remember Goliad!" others echoed.

Texas leaders sent Sam orders. "Fight Santa Anna! Defend Texas!"

But Sam's army was on the move! Would they retreat? Would they fight Santa Anna?

Only Sam Houston knew.

Then Santa Anna burned Harrisburg.

"Fight!" Texas leaders ordered again.

Still Sam marched toward the Sabine River. Would Sam Houston desert Texas? Even Sam's soldiers wondered. Would Sam Houston ever stop and fight?

Then Sam gave his orders. "Trust in God!" he said. "And remember the Alamo!"

Quickly, the army crossed Buffalo Bayou. Sam sent out his scouts. "Burn Vince's bridge!" he ordered. Now the army had no way to escape.

VICTORY!

Santa Anna's camp lay just across the plains. It was near the San Jacinto River.

Silently, Sam's soldiers rolled out two cannons. They were called the "Twin Sisters."

But Sam's soldiers had little ammunition. They loaded the cannons with horseshoes.

Now they were ready to fight!

Sam Houston mounted his horse. Saracen snorted. He pawed the ground. Even Sam Houston's horse was ready for battle.

Soldiers pushed the Twin Sisters out. A drum rolled. Fifes played.

Sam Houston raised his sword. Down the plains of San Jacinto the Texans roared!

"Remember the Alamo!" they yelled. "Remember Goliad!"

The Mexicans were in their tents. They were not ready to fight.

Suddenly, they heard horses. They heard soldiers yelling. They heard guns firing.

They hurried for their guns. They grabbed knives. But the Texans were too quick.

Sam waved his hat. The Texans charged.

Then Sam felt pain in his leg. He was shot. His boot filled with blood.

Saracen was shot too. He fell dead. But Sam grabbed another horse and fought on.

The Texans fought harder and harder. Soon the Mexican army broke up and ran. Santa Anna tried to escape. But the Texans captured him.

Sam Houston and his army won the Battle of San Jacinto.

But Sam's leg hurt. His wound was deep. He went to New Orleans. There he could see a doctor.

People greeted him. They waved flags. "Hooray for Sam Houston!" they shouted. "Hooray for the hero of San Jacinto!"

A NEW REPUBLIC

Texas no longer belonged to Mexico. Now Texas was free.

Texans could make their own laws. They could govern themselves. They made a new republic.

Some Texans wanted to join the United States. Others wanted to remain a republic.

But Texans agreed on one thing. They wanted Sam Houston to be their leader.

Sam served two terms as president of Texas. He made peace with the Indians. He tried to keep Texas out of debt.

Sam wrote to an old friend in Washington. He wanted President Jackson to make Texas part of the United States.

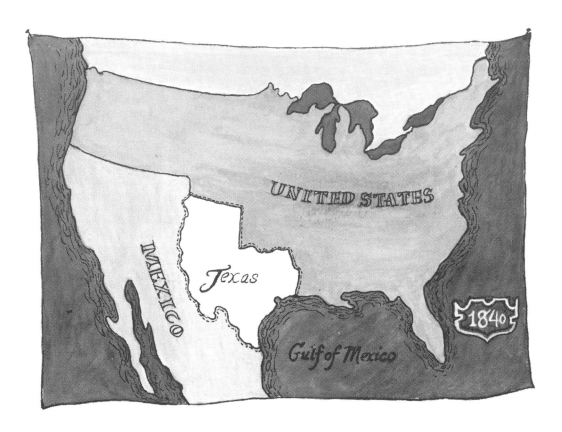

Sam Houston went to visit Alabama. He wanted people to come to Texas. He wanted people to buy land.

There he met Margaret Lea. She was very beautiful. She wrote poetry and played the piano.

Margaret and Sam fell in love. Soon they were married.

A Home for Sam

Margaret and Sam were very happy. They had their first child. They named him Sam too. Soon young Sam had a little sister. She was named Nannie.

Sam built Margaret a house. She called it their "Woodland Home."

Margaret was happy at home. She played her piano. She read stories to the children.

Sam loved home too. He liked to see his children climb trees and run in the fields. He liked to work in his law office. People came to see him. He told them stories of the Battle of San Jacinto.

But Sam loved to make speeches too. He liked being in government.

Now Texas was part of the United States. Many Texans wanted Sam to go to Washington. They wanted him to be their senator.

SAM HOUSTON — SENATOR

Sam was elected. He kissed Margaret and the children goodbye. Sam Houston was off to Washington.

United States senators wore black suits. But not Sam Houston. He often wore satin vests. But his favorite one was made of leopard skin.

Sometimes he wore an Indian blanket. What a sight Sam was! People wrote stories about the senator from Texas.

In the Senate he put his feet on his desk. Often he would whittle toys for his children.

Sam Houston also made many speeches. He talked about Texas. He talked about the United States. He loved them both.

But he missed Margaret. He missed his children too. And he missed Texas.

HOME TO TEXAS

Sam decided to run for governor. Then he could go home to Texas. But he lost.

Then he ran again and won. He and Margaret packed their yellow coach. They loaded their furniture. In climbed the children.

The Houstons were off to Austin!

Austin was the capital of Texas. The Houstons lived in the governor's mansion. Their son Temple Lea was born there.

But the United States was at war. Texas had to decide. Would they join the South? Would they fight in the Civil War?

A Hard Choice

Texans voted. They joined the South. They would fight the North.

But Sam was sad. He had fought for the United States. He wanted Texas in the Union.

Now Texas was leaving the Union. Sam would not vote to leave the United States. He could no longer be governor of Texas.

Sam and Margaret went home to Huntsville. They lived in Steamboat House. Their son Sam marched off to war. He fought for the South.

Young Sam was wounded but not killed. Sam and Margaret were proud of him.

A Hero's Death

Sam Houston still made speeches. But he was old and tired.

One day he came home ill. Margaret cared for him. But he did not get well.

On July 26, 1863, Sam's children stood by his bed. Margaret held Sam's hand.

"Texas! Margaret! Margaret!" Sam said. Those were his last words. The hero of San Jacinto died.

Texans did not forget Sam Houston. They remember him each year on March 2nd. It is Sam Houston's birthday. It is also Texas Independence Day.

Texans remember Senator Sam Houston. They remember Governor Sam Houston. And they remember Sam Houston — the hero of San Jacinto.

Words to Know

adventure	president	governor	echo
militia	Congress	niece	wonder
customers	prisoner	choice	ammunition
musket	settler	exciting	fife
ensign	retreat	law	poetry
split-log	plains	ruler	senator
ramparts	horseshoe	declare	whittle
buckskin	republic	desert	capital
government	speech	drill	mansion
promise	elect	supplies	Union
lawyer	duel	charge	civil
public office	hero	fort	vote
destiny	breeches	freedom	independence

Books About Sam Houston

Author, *Title*, Publisher

Flanagan, *Sam Houston's Texas*, University of Texas

Friend, *Sam Houston, the Great Designer*, University of Texas

Fritz, *Make Way for Sam Houston*, Putnam

Gregory and Strickland, *Sam Houston with the Cherokees*, University of Texas

Hopewell, *Sam Houston, Man of Destiny*, Eakin

Kennedy, *Sam Houston and the Senate*, Jenkins

James, *The Raven*, Mockingbird Books

James, *Six Feet Six*, Bobbs-Merrill

Seale, *Sam Houston's Wife*, University of Oklahoma

Wellman, *Magnificent Destiny*, Doubleday